SOMETHING EXTRAORDINARY

Celebrating Our Relief Society Sisterhood

Deseret Book Company
Salt Lake City, Utah

©1992 Deseret Book Company

All rights reserved. No part of this book may be reproduced in any form or by any means without permission in writing from the publisher, Deseret Book Company, P.O. Box 30178, Salt Lake City, Utah 84130.

Deseret Book is a registered trademark of Deseret Book Company.

Library of Congress Cataloging-in-Publication Data

Something extraordinary : celebrating our Relief Society sisterhood.
    p. cm.
    ISBN 0-87579-478-5. — ISBN 0-87579-592-7 (pbk.)
      1. Relief Society (The Church of Jesus Christ of Latter-day Saints)—
Pictorial works. 2. Women, Mormon—Pictorial works. I. Relief
Society (The Church of Jesus Christ of Latter-day Saints)
    BX8643.W4S65 1992
    267'.449332—dc20   91-36519
                                            CIP

ISBN 0-87579-478-5 (hardback edition)   ISBN 0-87579-592-7 (paperback edition)

Printed in the United States of America

10 9 8 7 6 5 4 3 2 1

Acknowledgments

The response to our request for photographs of Latter-day Saint women was overwhelming and gratifying. As we reviewed more than 4,250 photographs from 630 individuals in fifty-seven countries, we wished that each of you could have joined us in looking through everything from professional work to snapshots to historical photos from sisters' treasured family albums. We enjoyed each photo and the story it told. Each wonderful face made us grateful to be part of the celebration of our Relief Society sisterhood.

The Sesquicentennial Photo Book Committee worked long hours for many months to gather and organize the photos. Heidi Swinton has been a devoted, enthusiastic, and visionary chair of an excellent committee composed of JoAn Bitton, Angelyn Hutchinson, Shauna Horne, and Melanie Shumway. Sheri Dew, committed and superb chair of Deseret Book's team, worked with Kent Ware, Suzanne Brady, Karmel Howell, Patti Taylor, and Linda Nimori. Their invaluable professional assistance brought this project to pass. Carol Clark and Cherry Silver, members of the Relief Society General Board, served as Relief Society liaisons. Carol Clark facilitated and coordinated every phase of the project along with Heidi Swinton and Sheri Dew.

We thank all who sent us entries and gratefully acknowledge the willingness of photographers and committee members to contribute without financial compensation. Such gifts typify the desire of Church members to serve our Heavenly Father and each other.

The quotations in this book come from the presidents of the Church and the general presidents of the Relief Society. The dates show the years during which the individuals served in their calling. Also included are quotations from the scriptures and from the mother of the Prophet Joseph Smith.

NETHERLANDS

AUSTRALIA/ZIMBABWE/GERMANY

UNITED STATES

I have often felt that a photograph of our dear sisters,
with the intelligent, god-like faces they possess,
would be a testimony to all the world
of the integrity of our people.

Heber J. Grant, 1918–1945

Relief Society Magazine, December 1930, page 680

CANADA

UNITED STATES

RUSSIA

UNITED STATES   PEGGY JELLINGHAUSEN

ARGENTINA

A MESSAGE FROM THE GENERAL

RELIEF SOCIETY GENERAL PRESIDENCY left to right: Chieko N. Okazaki, first counselor; Elaine L. Jack, president; Aileen H. Clyde, second counselor

At the founding of Relief Society on 17 March 1842, Emma Smith, wife of the Prophet Joseph Smith and the Relief Society's first president, told her sisters:

We are going to do something extraordinary . . .
we expect extraordinary occasions and pressing calls.

Something Extraordinary: Celebrating Our Relief Society Sisterhood *joyously demonstrates the unity and diversity of Relief Society members throughout the world. The women seen herein are all Relief Society members.*

PRESIDENCY OF THE RELIEF SOCIETY

Together, their faces create a portrait of our sisterhood—beautiful, spiritual, lively, and gloriously disparate. This photobook is a lasting tribute to the spirit of Latter-day Saint women, which is the spirit of Relief Society.

We entitled the book Something Extraordinary *because we find the women of Zion to be just that. As we celebrate the Relief Society Sesquicentennial, we celebrate much more than 150 years of Relief Society as an organization. We celebrate our sisters—the daughters of God, the women of Zion, the Saints in these latter days. We have never found anything more inspiring than the gospel exemplified in the countenances and lives of these fine women.*

We have never had greater reason to rejoice than we have now, joined together three million strong across the neighborhoods and continents of this world. We celebrate through Something Extraordinary *because of who we are, what we believe, and what each Relief Society sister does daily.*

We hope that as you look through the small pictures in this book, you will see a big picture, a portrait of an organization of women bonded together in the greatest of all causes. We hope you will rejoice and recommit as you see the faces of our sisters illuminated by the gospel of Jesus Christ. We hope you will sense the value of your own life and better understand that what you are and what you do matter.

In the 150 years since Relief Society began, the women of Zion have done many things extraordinary . . .

. . . and done them extraordinarily well. Relief Society has grown steadily in numbers and influence.

GUATEMALA

CRAIG DIMOND

SWEDEN

PEGGY JELLINGHAUSEN

AUSTRALIA

CAROL CLARK

Relief Society is the sum of the righteousness of each sister.

GHANA

AUSTRALIA

UNITED STATES

BARBADOS

A word or two in relation to the Relief society. This is an organization that was established by the Prophet Joseph Smith. It is, therefore, the oldest auxiliary organization of the Church and it is of the first importance. It has not only to deal with the necessities of the poor, the sick and the needy, but a part of its duty—and the larger part, too—is to look after the spiritual welfare and salvation of the mothers and daughters of Zion; to see that none is neglected, but that all are guarded against misfortune, calamity, the powers of darkness, and the evils that threaten them in the world.

Joseph F. Smith, 1901–1918

In Conference Report, April 1906, page 3

AUSTRIA

HONG KONG

FRANCE

NIGERIA

D. ALSTON

Your life is a testament to your testimony of our Savior, Jesus Christ.

UNITED STATES

You are something extraordinary.

CZECHOSLOVAKIA

CRAIG DIMOND

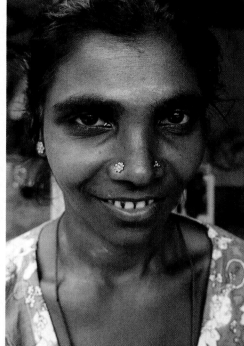

SINGAPORE

J MALAN HESLOP

UNITED STATES

MELANIE SHUMWAY

He inviteth them all to come unto him
and partake of his goodness.

2 Nephi 26:33

12

CANADA

CATHERINE DE VOS

MARSHALL ISLANDS

HELEN CLAIRE SIEVERS

UNITED STATES

JOAN BITTON

We see the light of Christ in your face.

UNITED STATES   CINDY BATEMAN   KOREA   J MALAN HESLOP   RUSSIA   MARGARET SMOOT   PHILIPPINES   CRAIG DIMOND

Have ye spiritually been born of God?
Have ye received his image in your countenances?
Alma 5:14

We see many evidences of your divine lineage as a daughter of God.

JAPAN

ENGLAND

UNITED STATES   FINLAND   UNITED STATES

A beautiful, modest, gracious woman is creation's masterpiece.
When to these virtues a woman possesses as guiding stars in her life righteousness
and godliness and an irresistible impulse and desire to make others happy,
no one will question if she be classed among those who are the truly great.

David O. McKay, 1951–1970

Funeral sermon for Emma Lucy Gates Bowen, 3 May 1951, in *Gospel Ideals*, Improvement Era, 1953, page 449

UNITED STATES

Your faithful living of the Lord's commandments weaves strength and stability into your life.

FINLAND

The women of the Church have an important work to do.
That work requires great strength of character, faith in the Lord Jesus Christ,
and a pure heart that will be a light unto the world and a bulwark of righteousness
against the darkness that covers the earth with contention and evil.

Barbara B. Smith, 1974–1984

Ensign, May 1984, page 30

Your steadfastness shows through every daily, loving act of charity.

GERMANY Relief Society members helping to build a meetinghouse

PARAGUAY

UNITED STATES

UNITED STATES

NEW ZEALAND

UNITED STATES

Without the
wonderful work
of the women
I realize
that the Church
would have been
a failure.

Heber J. Grant,
1918–1945

Relief Society Magazine,
June 1930, page 335

Across the continents we join hands to celebrate our sisterhood.

BARBARA W. WINDER

CZECHOSLOVAKIA

YOUNG CHUL KIM

KOREA

GERMANY

SOUTH AFRICA

BARB CHRISTIANSEN

COLOMBIA

JOANN H. THOMAS

BARBADOS

PHILIPPINES

RICHARD M. ROMNEY

We celebrate our relationships with the Lord and with each other.

AUSTRIA

UNITED STATES

JED CLARK

UNITED STATES

CLAIRE FIELD

UNITED STATES   SWITZERLAND

We celebrate the grandeur of your heart, your convictions, and your contributions.

AUSTRALIA

HAITI

W e celebrate that you and all the sisters of Relief Society demonstrate how women . . .

ECUADOR homemaking meeting

IVANI CABRAL

. . . united in loving service can be a force for good in every corner of our challenging world.

JAPAN homemaking meeting

LDS CHURCH HISTORICAL LIBRARY

UNITED STATES homemaking meeting

PHYLLIS TODD

NIGERIA homemaking meeting

WILLIAM ANGEL

It is natural for females to have feelings of charity and benevolence.
You are now placed in a situation in which you can act
according to those sympathies which God has planted in your bosoms.
If you live up to these principles, how great and glorious
will be your reward in the celestial kingdom!

Joseph Smith, 1830–1844

History of the Church, 4:605

SINGAPORE
BARBARA HONG

UNITED STATES
JED CLARK

PHILIPPINES
MARY ELLEN EDMUNDS

We join together as women of different nations, ages, experience, and color.

MAURITIUS

TRANSKEI, SOUTH AFRICA
ANN LAEMMLEN LEWIS

UNITED STATES
BONNIE NIELSON

We, being many, are one . . . in Christ.

Romans 12:5

Organize yourselves; prepare every needful thing.

Doctrine and Covenants 88:119

We make our homes in every climate and in every situation throughout 135 countries and territories.

KOREA

TRANSKEI, SOUTH AFRICA

UNITED STATES

VIETNAM

Though our languages and our circumstances differ, we are knit together by our desires to live righteously.

UNITED STATES

AUSTRIA

UNITED STATES

UNITED STATES

UNITED STATES

There should be no contention one with another, but . . . they should look forward
with one eye, having one faith and one baptism, having their hearts knit together in unity
and in love one towards another. . . . And thus they became the children of God.

Mosiah 18:21–22

DENMARK

We find meaning in our daily lives. We find purpose as we live the truths that lead to eternal life.

RUSSIA The Moscow Branch Relief Society

The Relief Society was organized by Joseph Smith by revelation, and has for its object
the building up of the Kingdom of God. It does not all depend upon the Elders of Israel
by any means. You are like ministering angels; you are aids to the bishops,
and a great many worthy people would suffer were it not for these organizations.
The responsibilities of building up this Kingdom rest alike upon the man and the woman. . . .
Let me say to the sisters of Zion, we cannot do without your assistance
in accomplishing this great work.

Wilford Woodruff, 1889–1898

Woman's Exponent, 15 July 1880, page 30

GUAM

BRAZIL

We rejoice in the covenants we make in the temple, the house of the Lord.

THAILAND

JAPAN

UNITED STATES

BRAZIL

HELEN BAY GIBBONS

Our sisters should be prepared to take their position in Zion. Our sisters are really one with us . . . ;
we operate together for the good of the whole, that we may be united together for time and all eternity.

John Taylor, 1880–1887

Woman's Exponent, 1 June 1879, page 248

UNITED STATES

We are happy to be linked eternally in righteousness as husbands and wives, sons and daughters of God.

UNITED STATES

GERMANY

UNITED STATES

Some think of happiness as a glamorous life of ease, luxury, and constant thrills;
but true marriage is based on a happiness that is more than that, one that
comes from giving, serving, sharing, sacrificing, and selflessness.

Spencer W. Kimball, 1973–1985

Marriage, Deseret Book, 1978, page 45

PHOTO ON PAGES 42-43
GUATEMALA
BY CRAIG DIMOND

We thank the Lord for the blessing of becoming covenant people.

Blessed are ye if ye shall believe in me and be baptized, . . . and know that I am.

3 Nephi 12:1

We thank Him for every good thing that comes to us because we are alive now.

FINLAND

AUSTRALIA

HONG KONG

TAHITI

UNITED STATES

Never have women had greater influence than in today's world. Never have the doors of opportunity opened wider for them. This is an inviting, exciting, challenging, and demanding period of time for women. It is a time rich in rewards if we keep our balance, learn the true values of life, and wisely determine priorities.

Belle S. Spafford, 1945–1974

A Woman's Reach, Deseret Book, 1974, page 21

SOUTH AFRICA

There is no sister so isolated, and her sphere so narrow but what she can do
a great deal towards establishing the Kingdom of God upon the earth.

Eliza R. Snow, 1866–1887

Woman's Exponent, 15 September 1873, page 62

UNITED STATES

MARK C. CANNON

RUSSIA

For we know that in this time together we can accomplish miracles.

BARBADOS

THAILAND

We serve with our brethren as partners, sharing a common purpose and goal.

UNITED STATES/KOREA/MEXICO

The Relief Society, as no other organization, is the "handmaiden" of the Priesthood of God.
In their joint responsibility in rendering compassionate service, they present a sort of "Father and Mother Image"
in the Kingdom of God to look after the needy and the unfortunate.

Harold B. Lee, 1972–1973

Relief Society Magazine, January 1969, page 12

Together we build the kingdom of God, one person and one home at a time.

AUSTRALIA

J MALAN HESLOP

UNITED STATES

HARRIET ARRINGTON

In these days, when needs and stresses are great, we rejoice in the quality and creativity of what you do.

TRANSKEI, SOUTH AFRICA

ANN LAEMMLEN LEWIS

UNITED STATES

PETE HOUDESHEL

UNITED STATES

CRAIG DIMOND

SAMOA

No greater heroine lives in today's world than the woman who is quietly doing her part.
Elaine L. Jack, 1990–

Ensign, November 1990, page 89

In villages, towns, and cities, you join your hearts and hands in Relief Societies, large and small, . . .

GUATEMALA Nahuala Ward Relief Society presidency

CAROL LEE HAWKINS

UNITED STATES Relief Society presidents, Ricks College

. . . to give the charity that never faileth.

ANADA Relief Society presidency, rtmouth Nova Scotia Stake

UNITED STATES Relief Society presidency, Brooklyn First Ward

AUSTRALIA Relief Society presidency, Enoggera Ward

UNITED STATES Ward Relief Society presidents, Oakland California Stake

UNITED STATES Relief Society presidency, Imperial First Ward

The work of Relief Society is focused on the pure and simple part of the gospel, . . .
to work with our "hearts knit together in unity and in love one towards another." (Mosiah 18:21.)
Barbara W. Winder, 1984–1990

Ensign, May 1990, page 76

You make "Charity Never Faileth" your personal motto.

UNITED STATES
SHARRI ROSVALL

UNITED STATES
PEGGY JELLINGHAUSEN

IRELAND
LILLIAN HENDERSON

MARSHALL ISLANDS
HELEN CLAIRE SIEVERS

NIGERIA
JACQUELINE WILSON

Women . . . have sympathy, imagination, patience, a spontaneous eagerness to help, and a warm good will, all of which are real assets and help them to find their way easily into the hearts of those who suffer.

Amy Brown Lyman, 1940–1945

Relief Society Magazine, March 1944, page 137

Charity is a part of life within your own home and within the schools, community centers, . . .

UNITED STATES

UNITED STATES

. . . church meetinghouses, businesses, and social agencies of this world where you serve.

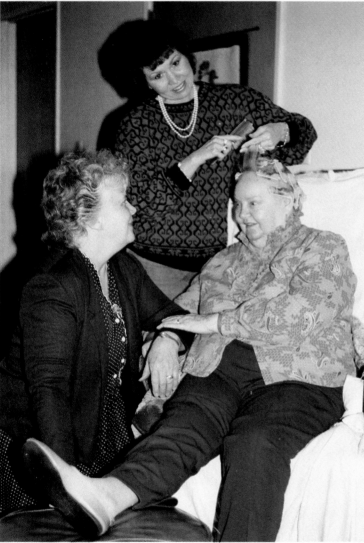

UNITED STATES

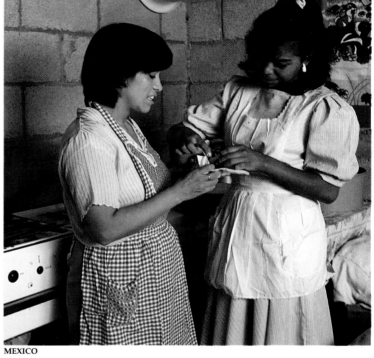

MEXICO

UNITED STATES

You are the quiet pioneers of this earth.

UNITED STATES

She . . . worketh willingly
with her hands. . . .

UNITED STATES

She stretcheth out her
hand to the poor. . . .

WHITECOTTON

UNITED STATES

She shall rejoice in
time to come. . . .

MEXICO

DENMARK

A woman that feareth the Lord,
she shall be praised.

Proverbs 31:13, 20, 25, 27, 30

She looketh well to the ways of her household. . . .

PHOTO ON PAGES 60-61
UNITED STATES
BY CRAIG LAW

You willingly teach the gospel, showing charity for all mankind.

Prepare ye the way of the Lord.

Matthew 3:3

You bless the world because you bless individuals.

ITALY

UNITED STATES

To be a mother in Israel in the full gospel sense is the highest reward that can come
into the life of a woman. This designation has a deep and significant meaning,
one that is far more than marrying and bearing children in this life,
great and important as that course is.

Joseph Fielding Smith, 1970–1972

Relief Society Magazine, December 1970, page 883

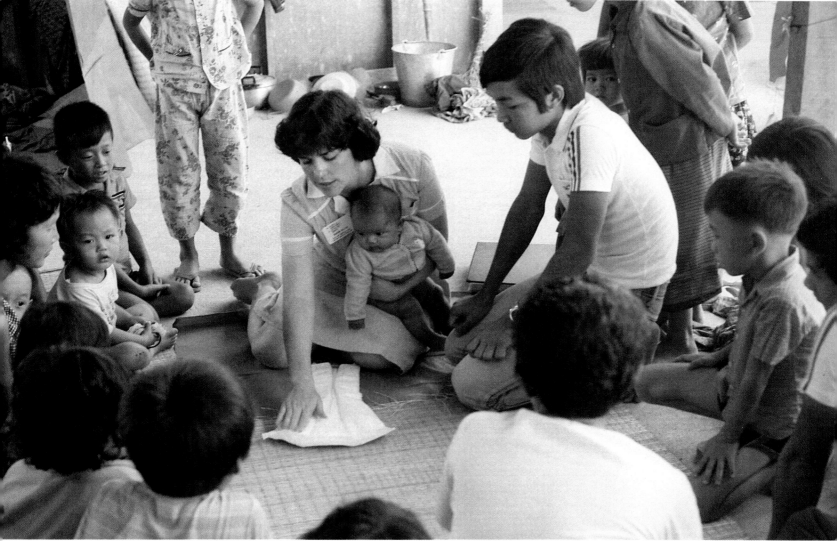

THAILAND

UNITED STATES

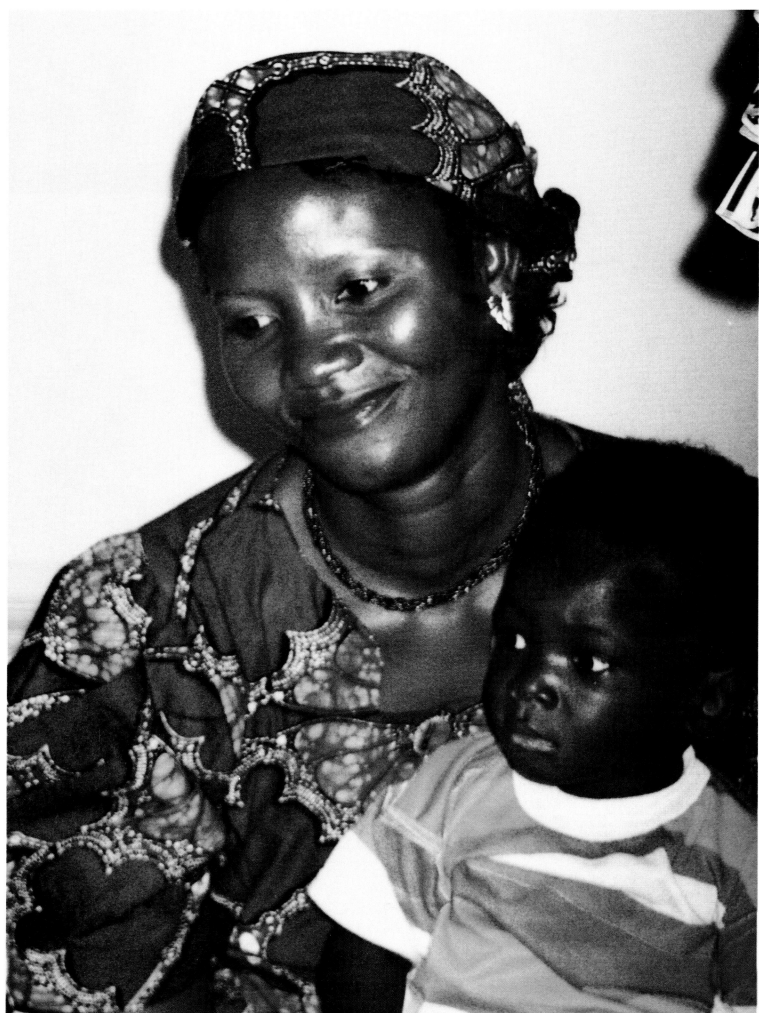

GHANA

CANADA

Your sensitivity, kindness, humor, and warmth enrich all whose lives you touch.

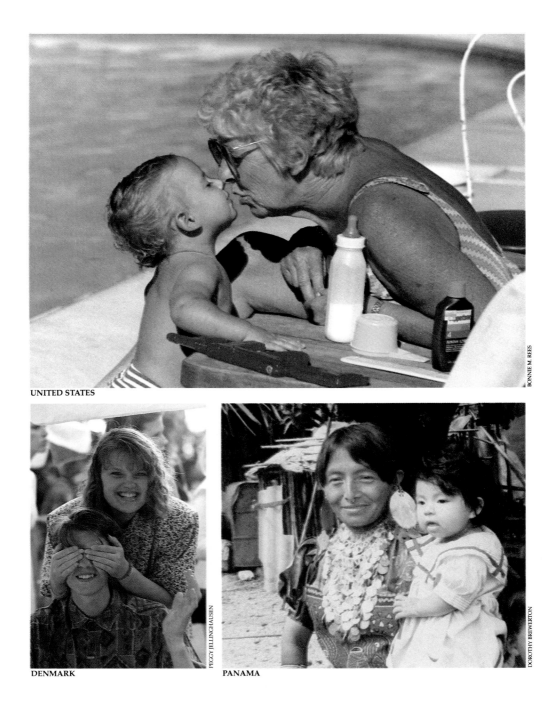

UNITED STATES

DENMARK

PANAMA

65

As a wife and mother, you bless generations.

HUNGARY

AUSTRIA

UNITED STATES

As the givers and the guardians of life
it is the task of women in the midst of any
and all exigencies and emergencies
to bring up the generation of tomorrow.

Amy Brown Lyman, 1940–1945

Women and the Home Today,
radio address delivered 14 March 1943, page [4]

UNITED STATES

In every type of family you live righteously.

ANN FLORENCE

UNITED STATES

CINDY BATEMAN

HONG KONG

NESTOR CURBELO

ARGENTINA

The family is one
of God's greatest fortresses
against the evils of our day.

Ezra Taft Benson,
1985–

Ensign, May 1986, page 43

Thou shalt live together in love.
Doctrine and Covenants 42:45

UNITED STATES

UNITED STATES

As sister, neighbor, teacher, friend, grandmother, colleague, and aunt, you lift so many others.

UNITED STATES

UNITED STATES

UNITED STATES

ENGLAND

Reap satisfaction in all the relationships you so carefully plant, tend, and nurture, over and over . . .

GERMANY

PEGGY TELLINGHAUSEN

CAROLYN SESSIONS ALLEN

UNITED STATES

JAMAICA

AFRICA

. . . sometimes through seasons of emotional drought or deluge.

JAPAN

RICHARD J. RICHARDSON

Create meaningful relationships as you visit and teach each other.

UNITED STATES

PEGGY JELLINGHAUSEN

ZAIRE

GROVER

UNITED STATES

MYRNA R. CONDIE

Visiting teaching . . . is an answer of Relief Society
to the commandment of our Heavenly Father,
"feed my sheep."

Belle S. Spafford, 1945–1974

Relief Society Magazine, March 1958, page 175

UNITED STATES

Love—and like—one another. Enjoy being together.

We must cherish one another, watch over one another, comfort one another
and gain instruction, that we may all sit down in heaven together.

Lucy Mack Smith

In *History of Relief Society, 1842–1966*, General Board of Relief Society, 1967, page 20

INDONESIA

MARY ELLEN EDMUNDS

UNITED STATES

AMY L. ENGAR

UNITED STATES

V. DANE L. ROGERS

UNITED STATES

TRILBA LINDSAY

UNITED STATES   SUZANNE KING

UNITED STATES   JULIA SADLEIR

Savor the large and the small satisfactions and challenges of each day. We know you are someone wonderful, . . .

NIGERIA

UNITED STATES   LAKESIDE REVIEW

. . . so even your smallest accomplishments have wonder in them too.

MEXICO

J MALAN HESLOP

POLAND Young Women

UNITED STATES Primary

CANADA Relief Society

As a Primary teacher, Young Women adviser, or Relief Society leader, you bless and teach the one.

MALAYSIA Relief Society

DARWIN AND ARLOA WHITAKER

PEGGY JELLINGHAUSEN

UNITED STATES left to right: Elaine L. Jack, Relief Society general president; Ardeth G. Kapp, Young Women general president; Michaelene P. Grassli, Primary general president

Stand fast in one spirit,
with one mind striving together
for the faith of the gospel.

Philippians 1:27

THAILAND

May you delight in life and laugh often!

For ye shall go
out with joy,
and be led forth
with peace:
the mountains
and the hills
shall break forth
before you
into singing,
and all the trees
of the field
shall clap
their hands.

Isaiah 55:12

UNITED STATES   MELANIE SHUMWAY

NIGERIA · JACQUELINE WILSON   UNITED STATES · MELANIE SHUMWAY   JAPAN · KIYOKO MITSUHASHI

Relish the excitement, adventure, and pleasures of each season of womanhood.

UNITED STATES

MARY ELLEN EDMUNDS

UNITED STATES

DEAN MADSEN

UNITED STATES

RALPH T. CLARK (DESERET NEWS)

UNITED STATES

CRAIG DIMOND

This is a joyous gospel! . . . I know that in the strength
of the Lord we can do all things required of us.

Elaine L. Jack, 1990–

Ensign, May 1990, page 78

UNITED STATES

JAPAN

May many things refresh you. May they bring you perspective and enjoyment.

GRAND CAYMAN ISLAND

ROBERT BORLAND

JAPAN

RICHARD J. RICHARDSON

SAMOA

J MALAN HESLOP

UNITED STATES

MARK PHILBRICK

UNITED STATES

TRUDY BECK

UNITED STATES

DESERET NEWS

Recreation and diversion are as necessary to our well-being
as the more serious pursuits of life.

Brigham Young, 1847–1877

Discourses of Brigham Young, Deseret Book, 1954, page 238

May yours be a heart devoid of divisiveness.

UNITED STATES

UNITED STATES

Consider conquering yourself rather than comparing yourself unfavorably to others.

UNITED STATES

DOUG WILLIAMS

CANADA

CONNIE STEED

NEW ZEALAND

CATRIENA WILKINSON

ENGLAND

I desire to impress on you daughters of God . . . that if this world is to endure, you must keep the faith.
If this world is to be happy, you will have to set the pace for that happiness. . . . If we are to maintain our physical
strength and mental power and spiritual joy, it will have to be on the Lord's terms.

George Albert Smith, 1945–1951

Relief Society Magazine, December 1945, page 719

Do what you can, and do it lovingly. The Lord asks that of you, and we ask nothing more.

PARAGUAY   NESTOR CURBELO

UNITED STATES   RICHARD L. LEE

GUATEMALA   CRAIG DIMOND

INDONESIA

GERMANY

MEXICO

UNITED STATES

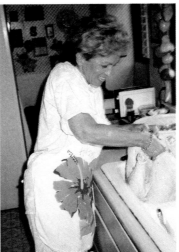

UNITED STATES

The Lord
doth give me
exceedingly
great joy
in the fruit
of my labors.

Alma 36:25

We rejoice in the wisdom, skill, and purpose you bring to your works.

NIGERIA

PAUL CHRISTIE

UNITED STATES

MELANIE SHUMWAY

JED CLARK

UNITED STATES

MELANIE SHUMWAY

UNITED STATES

MARK C. CANNON

UNITED STATES

PEGGY JELLINGHAUSEN

UNITED STATES

SWITZERLAND

HELEN RINGGER

UNITED STATES

UNITED STATES

We have been given such blessings as have never been given to women in any other age,
and we should in every way endeavor to live up to them.

Clarissa S. Williams, 1921–1928

Relief Society Magazine, December 1921, page 696

We rejoice in the many ways you make this world a better place.

LIBERIA

STELLA CUNNINGHAM

AUSTRALIA

JAN SCHMIDT

UNITED STATES

SHAUNA HORNE

TAHITI

JAYNANN WENDT

UNITED STATES

J MALAN HESLOP

Learn all you can about the glories of the Lord.

GUATEMALA

It is plainly necessary that women as well as men,
cease not while life lasts to study diligently,
for the knowledge which is of greatest worth.

Bathsheba W. Smith, 1901–1910

Woman's Exponent, January 1906, page 41

ARGENTINA

Search and ponder the words of life.

UNITED STATES

I want the sisters to study the scriptures and
become familiar with the Bible and the Book of Mormon.
Let them be holy books unto you.
Emmeline B. Wells, 1910–1921

Relief Society Magazine, August 1919, page 439

Pray from the depth of your gratitude and of your need.

UNITED STATES

UNITED STATES

It seems to me that the women of the Latter-day Saints
should have more gratitude than anybody else in the world
for the restoration of the gospel.

Louise Y. Robison, 1928–1939

Relief Society Magazine, June 1929, page 311

UNITED STATES

UNITED STATES

MELANIE SHUMWAY

Every good gift cometh of Christ.
Moroni 10:18

AUSTRALIA

J MALAN HESLOP

Develop your unique gifts and abilities, remembering that your talents are some of your best gifts from God.

GERMANY

PEGGY JELLINGHAUSEN

UNITED STATES

ANN FLORENCE

BELGIUM

PEGGY JELLINGHAUSEN

Seek and find knowledge all around you.

MEXICO

POLAND

ITALY

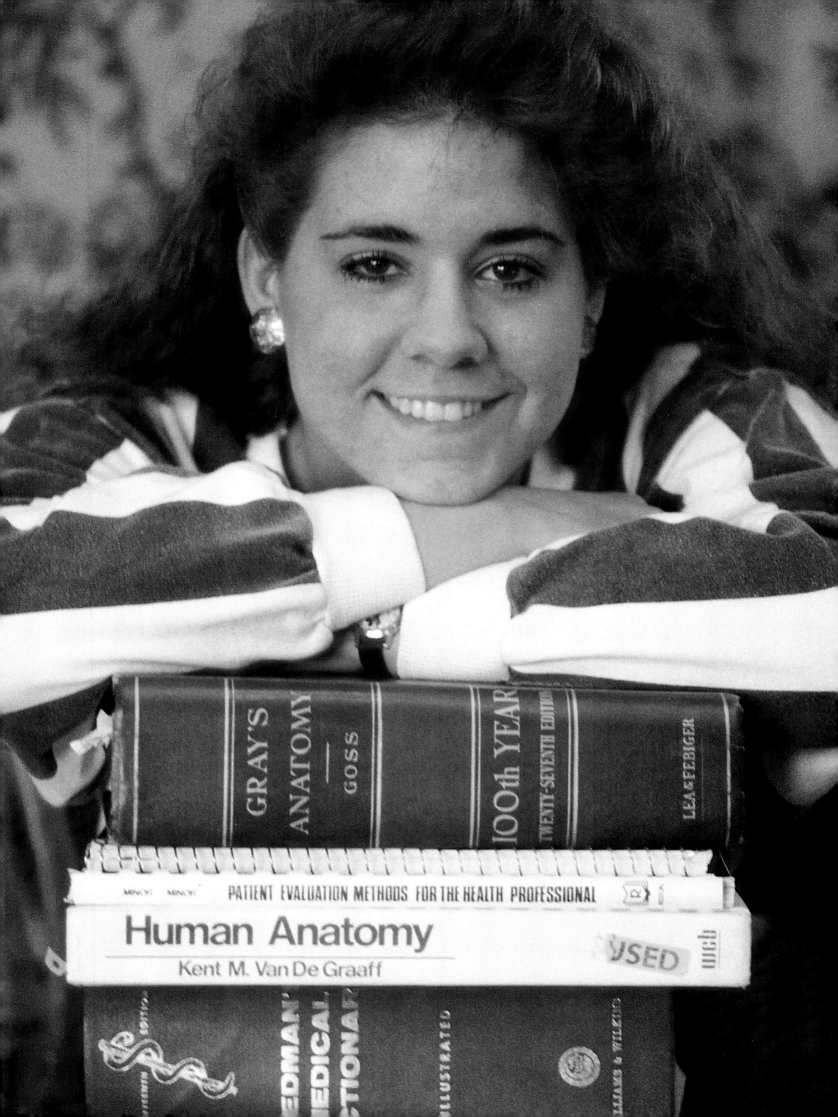

JAPAN early-morning seminary class

KOSUGI SHIBU

UNITED STATES

CRAIG LAW

UNITED STATES

BONNIE NIELSON

DOMINICAN REPUBLIC

UNITED STATES

Then teach, so others may learn. And learn, so others may teach.

INDIA

PEOPLE'S REPUBLIC OF CHINA

MEXICO

UNITED STATES   JED CLARK

Add to your faith virtue;
and to virtue knowledge.

2 Peter 1:5

Relish all the wondrous diversity of people, places, and things.

SHARON FRANKLIN-RAHKONEN

UNITED STATES

PEGGY JELLINGHAUSEN

UNITED STATES

SHIRLEY JENSEN HICKS

NIGERIA

NIGERIA

SHAUNA HORNE

UNITED STATES

108

Cultivate courage, so you may live serenely and well.

BOLIVIA

I can testify that there are no purer and more God-fearing women in the world than are to be found within the ranks of the Relief Society.

Lorenzo Snow, 1898–1901

Deseret Evening News, 9 July 1901, page 1

MARY ELLEN EDMUNDS

ENGLAND

ANNE BRADSHAW

BARBARA W. WINDER

CZECHOSLOVAKIA

AUSTRALIA

CAROL CLARK

INDONESIA

ROBERT W. HOUGHTON

111

When your challenges come, thank the Lord for your knowledge that He lives and feel peace, knowing He cares for you.

When thou passest through the waters, I will be with thee;
and through the rivers, they shall not overflow thee:
when thou walkest through the fire, thou shalt not be burned;
neither shall the flame kindle upon thee.
For I am the Lord thy God, the Holy One of Israel,
thy Saviour.

Isaiah 43:2–3

112

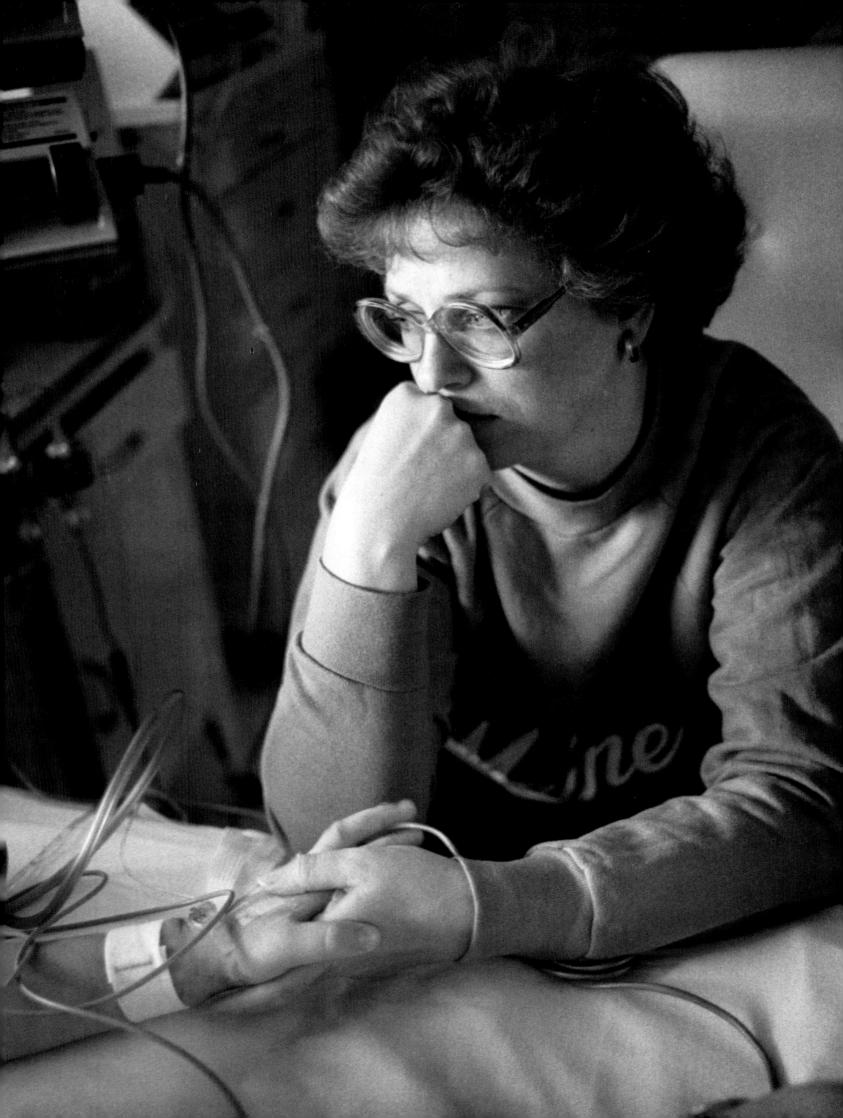

JAPAN

RICHARD J RICHARDSON

RUSSIA

CRAIG DIMOND

UNITED STATES

JOE HALLMAN

We love you. We pray that the great truths of the gospel will resonate in your soul . . .

UNITED STATES

CRAIG DIMOND

AUSTRALIA   FITZGERALD

MARSHALL ISLANDS   HELEN CLAIRE SIEVERS

ENGLAND   J MALAN HESLOP

UNITED STATES   JED CLARK

. . . in times of trial or triumph and through all the days in between.

CZECHOSLOVAKIA   PEGGY JELLINGHAUSEN

UNITED STATES/MEXICO   JED CLARK

May we as women of Zion, ever know and honor our true position,
and continue to grow in grace, and abound in good works,
until He whose right it is to reign shall come.

Zina D. H. Young, 1888–1901

Woman's Exponent, 15 April 1889, page 173

NIGERIA

We pray that you will live so the Spirit of the Lord will abide in your heart and in your home.

DOMINICAN REPUBLIC

GUATEMALA

CRAIG DIMOND

UNITED STATES/SAMOA

PEGGY JELLINGHAUSEN

SHERI DEW

UNITED STATES

117

UNITED STATES   CZECHOSLOVAKIA   UNITED STATES

With all our hearts we hope you will feel to thank our Heavenly Father . . .

BRAZIL

GERMANY

AUSTRIA

UNITED STATES

... for the life and mission of our Savior Jesus Christ, for your testimony, and for His many gifts to you.

UNITED STATES

GUATEMALA

119

UNITED STATES CRAIG LAW

UNITED STATES RICHARD M. ROMNEY

GERMANY PEGGY JELLINGHAUSEN

Most of all, we hope you feel loved, knowing that you are what we celebrate . . .

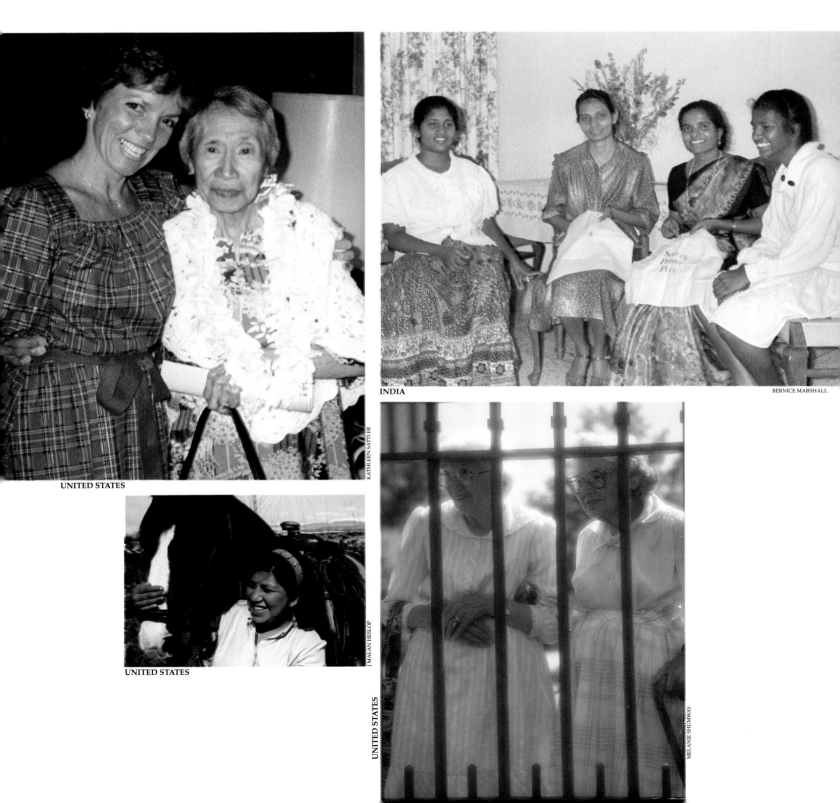

UNITED STATES KATHLEEN SATTLER

INDIA BERNICE MARSHALL

UNITED STATES J MALAN HESLOP

UNITED STATES MELANIE SHUMWAY

HAITI

PHILIPPINES

MARY ELLEN EDMUNDS

. . . for to us you are truly something extraordinary.

POLAND

PEGGY JELLINGHAUSEN

UNITED STATES

PEGGY JELLINGHAUSEN

GHANA

JOSEPH JACK

JAPAN

SUMIKO KUMAKURA

BOLIVIA

J MALAN HESLOP

GERMANY

PEGGY JELLINGHAUSEN

UNITED STATES

And now, after the many testimonies which have been given of him,
this is the testimony, last of all, which we give of him:
That he lives!

Doctrine and Covenants 76:22